CONTENTS

⚙ **TECH-TALK**

Look for the cog and blue box for explanations of technical terms.

◉ **EYE-VIEW**

Look for the eye and yellow box for eyewitness accounts.

DAWN OF RACING

▲ Refuelling a Fiat racing car in 1912.

There have been races since the early days of motoring, more than 100 years ago.

The first big motor race was held in 1895, from Paris to Bordeaux and back, in France. The winner drove at just 24 km/h. This may seem slow, but at that time most roads between cities were little more than muddy and bumpy tracks.

MONSTER ⚙ MACHINES

RACING CARS

DAVID JEFFERIS

NEWCASTLE-UNDER-LYME
COLLEGE LEARNING
RESOURCES

Belitha Press

▲ The best rally cars have four-wheel drive, which means that power is sent to all four wheels. This helps a car to keep going in bad conditions.

First published in Great Britain in 2001 by Belitha Press Limited, an imprint of Chrysalis Books plc, 64 Brewery Road, London N7 9NT

Paperback edition first published in 2002

Copyright © David Jefferis/Alpha Communications 2001

Educational advisor Julie Stapleton
Design and editorial production Alpha Communications
Picture research Kay Rowley

ISBN 1 84138 189 6 (hardback)
ISBN 1 84138 385 6 (paperback)

Printed in Hong Kong.

10 9 8 7 6 5 4 3 2 1 (hardback)
10 9 8 7 6 5 4 3 2 1 (paperback)

British Library Cataloguing in Publication Data for this book is available from the British Library.

Acknowledgements
We wish to thank the following individuals and organizations for their help and assistance and for supplying material in their collections:
Jorge Alburquerque, All-Sport Photographic Ltd, Tim Andrew, Alpha Archive, Simon Bruty, Jeremy Davey/SSC Programme Ltd, Jon Ferrey, Robert Laberge, LAT Photographic, Ken Levine, McKlein, Gavin Page, Mike Powell, Tamiya Model Co

✿ BODYWORK SECRETS

Racing cars are built around a strong body, called a monocoque. It protects the driver in a crash, and supports parts such as the engine and wheels. You don't normally see the monocoque, as it is hidden behind outer panels. This racing car is stripped down, before a race. For racing, the colourful outer panels will be fixed with screws and fasteners.

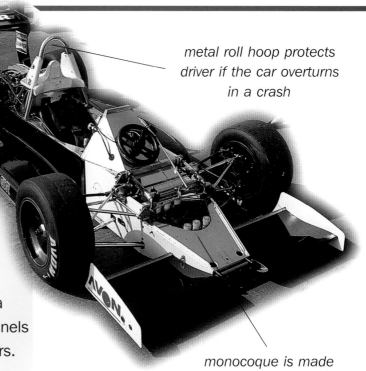

metal roll hoop protects driver if the car overturns in a crash

monocoque is made of light but strong aluminium

Today, that early race would be called a rally, an event that is still popular. Even so, most car racing today takes place on specially-built tracks. The most important races are called Grand Prix, which are the French words for 'big prize'.

Different kinds of racing are divided into formulas. These are strict rules that say how cars should be built – for instance, what their size, weight and power should be. Officials, called scrutineers, check cars before every race.

◀ The driver lies almost flat in the car, with just his helmet sticking out of the cockpit.

GRAND PRIX RACER

Racing cars are built with one thing in mind, to win races. So designers work hard to create cars that are light in weight and have powerful engines.

▲▼ In Formula 1 racers, the engine is placed low behind the driver, hidden inside the body panels. It powers the back wheels.

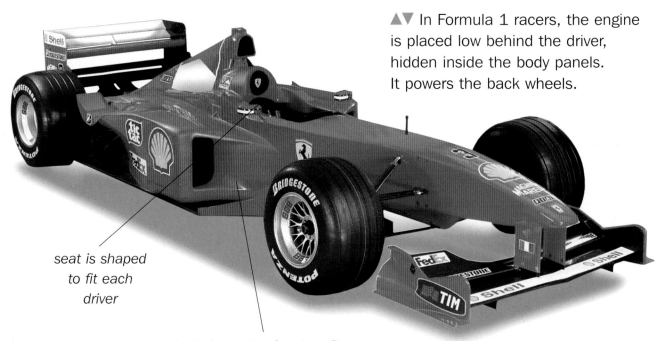

seat is shaped to fit each driver

body is made of carbon fibre, which is light but very strong

Formula 1 cars are built around a light but strong body, called a monocoque. The word comes from the French for 'single shell', because it is built in one unit.

Joined to the monocoque ar the engine, wheels and suspension. Aerofoil 'wings' at the front and back keep the car steady when it is being driven at high speed.

▶ Italy's Ferrari is the only Formula 1 car-maker that also makes its own engines. Most racing teams have their car and engine supplied by different companies.

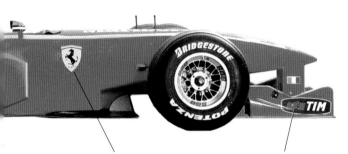

Ferrari uses a black horse as its company badge

the front wing pushes down, to help keep the car on the track

▼ Wide tyres give lots of grip for turning corners at high speed. The small wing on top of the car has a tiny video camera inside, so TV viewers can see a driver's view of the race.

PIT STOP

▲ A car's cockpit is a tight fit. Seat belts keep drivers in place.

The pits are areas where racing cars are serviced and refuelled. In most races, cars need two or three pit stops. Long-distance races may need more.

▼ Pit crew refuel a BMW in less than eight seconds.

Pit stops have to be lightning-fast, and an unexpected delay may lose a driver the race. In just a few seconds – between six and nine is normal – a trained pit-crew can top up the fuel tank, change the tyres, check the engine and wipe clean the driver's helmet.

pipe from fuel tank in the pits

▲ Air tanks blow up tyres very quickly. Here, a trolley is loaded, ready for a race.

✿ CHOOSING TYRES

Racing tyres come in two main types, one sort for dry tracks, the other for wet weather. Wet tyres have a groove-pattern cut into the rubber surface, so that water can drain away quickly. Dry tyres are smooth, although Formula 1 tyres now have four deep grooves. This is for safety – to slow the cars down in corners.

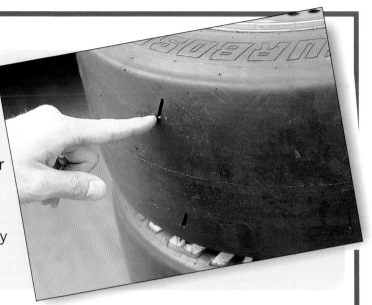

OVAL TRACK STARS

Stock car racing in the US takes place on wide, oval tracks. Cars are based on saloon cars, but big engines turn them into monster racing machines.

▲ US stock racers are based on saloon cars.

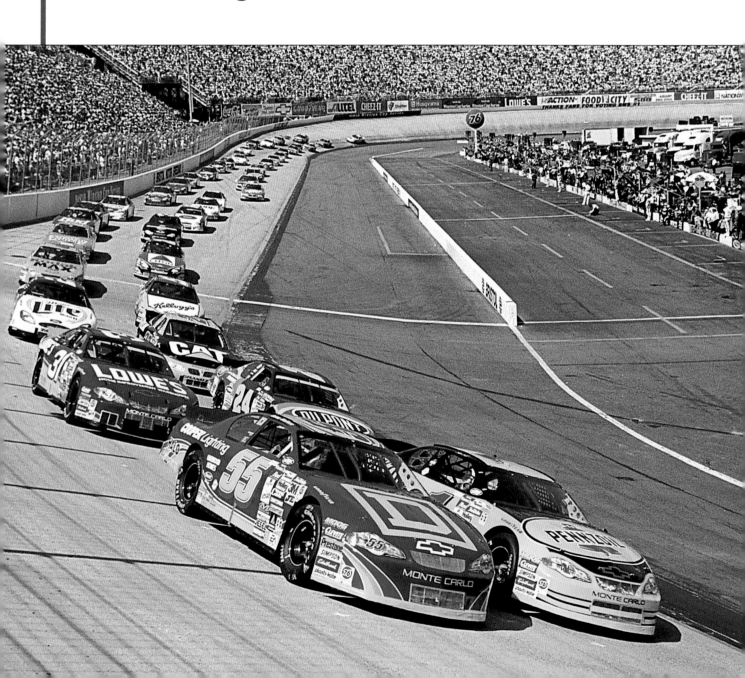

◉ THUNDER IN THE SUN

'Engine noise at a race often feels loud enough to blow your ears off! Pit crew use ear-defenders to avoid hearing damage – defenders cut sound by more than half. The pit chief has a radio, so he can talk to the driver at any time.' *Pit crew member*

pit crew wear ear defenders

US stock car racing is a big test of drivers and cars. Races often last several hours. Regular pit stops and slow-downs to clear away crashed cars add to the thrills.

Wide tracks give drivers room to overtake each other many times during a race. This is unlike Formula 1 races, where narrower tracks and more corners make overtaking less common.

◀ A Pontiac stock car reaches 300 km/h on the straights.

◀ A huge crowd looks on as cars line up for the start at the US Bristol Motor Speedway.

⚙ WHY DO SPEEDWAYS HAVE SLOPING CORNERS?

Stock car circuits have banked (sloping) corners, so drivers can keep going fast. On a flat track, cars have to slow down much more for corners. If a driver takes a bend too fast, the car's tyres will lose their grip and the car may slide, out of control. Banking reduces sideways slip when cornering.

24-HOUR RACERS

The most famous long-distance race is held at Le Mans, in France. Every year teams compete in a race that lasts for 24 hours.

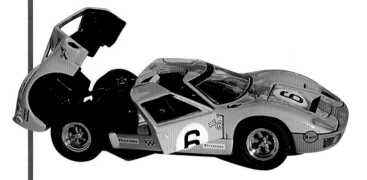

◀ The Ford GT40 won Le Mans three years running in the 1960s. The rear opened so pit crew could service the engine easily.

▼ Le Mans racing cars usually look similar. There is central cockpit, with the engine behind. Powerful lights are needed at night.

Le Mans is one of motor sport's toughest challenges. The cars race flat-out for the entire course, and leading cars may cover more than 5000 km from start to finish. Many cars break down and never finish at all.

Bad weather is another enemy, especially heavy rain. Dry-weather tyres have little grip in the wet, so it is easy to slide off the track.

👁 24 HOURS OF SPEED AND POWER

'Le Mans is somewhere every motor race fan should go, at least once. The track is made of ordinary roads, which are closed for the event. The noise and smell of the cars is something you never get anywhere else. Whatever the weather (sometimes it pours with rain) the cars hurtle along at 400 km/h or more. And there is a funfair that you can visit in the evening!' *Le Mans visitor*

It is nearly sunset as a car roars under a footbridge at Le Mans. Racing carries on all through the night. On straight parts of the circuit, the fastest cars go at about 400 km/h.

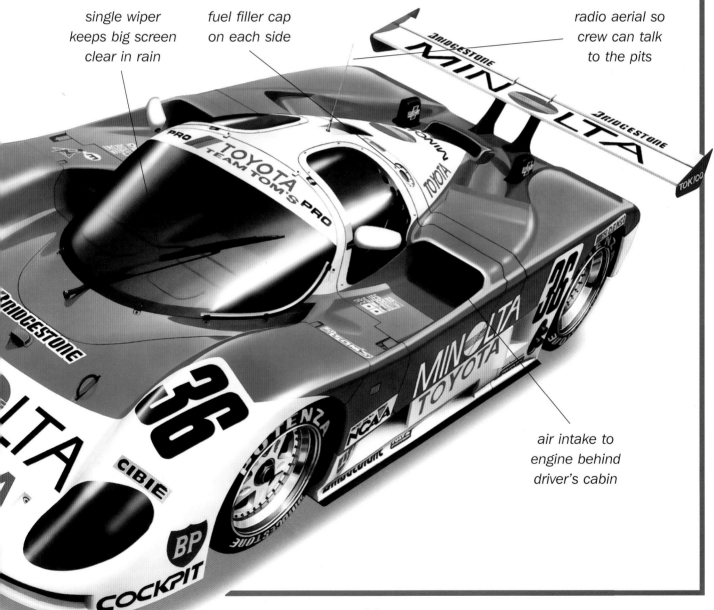

single wiper keeps big screen clear in rain

fuel filler cap on each side

radio aerial so crew can talk to the pits

air intake to engine behind driver's cabin

RALLY CHAMPIONS

spare tyres
carried on roof

▲ Drivers in the small but fast Austin Mini won the Monte Carlo rally three times in the 1960s.

Rally drivers race against the clock on courses that are made up of road and off-road sections. The biggest rallies cover thousands of kilometres.

The World Rally Championship is the most important rallying event. Drivers compete in rallies held in 14 countries across the world. Courses range from ice and snow in Finland to heat and dust in Africa.

The last race is in November, when the winner is declared. There is a break until January, and the Championship starts again.

⚙ KEEPING A GRIP

The fastest rally cars are usually fitted with four-wheel drive. This means that all four wheels are powered from the engine, so drivers can take turns quicker and get out of muddy spots more easily. If one or two wheels get stuck, the other ones can power the car out of trouble.

► People look on as a rally car hurtles around a hair-pin bend. Only top drivers get round tight corners like this without losing too much speed.

▼ A Spanish rally car throws up dust during the 1999 Safari Rally in Kenya. A metal grill at the front protects the engine from flying stones.

THE NAME GAME

Motor racing is big business. Many companies advertise by having their names painted on the cars. A company pays a racing team for this.

Big companies often back a racing team with money. In exchange the team advertises the company on their cars. This is called sponsorship. A top-class Formula One team needs more than £30 million a year to compete, so sponsorship is very important. And because racing is a worldwide sport, it is a good way of advertising to millions of people.

▲ The size of a sponsor's name depends on the money donated!

👁 RACING BEFORE ADVERTS
'When my grandad used to watch racing, back in the 1950s, each country had its own colour – Italy red, France blue, the US white with blue stripes, Britain dark green, and so on. It was a simple system, but they are more fun to look at today.' *Race enthusiast*

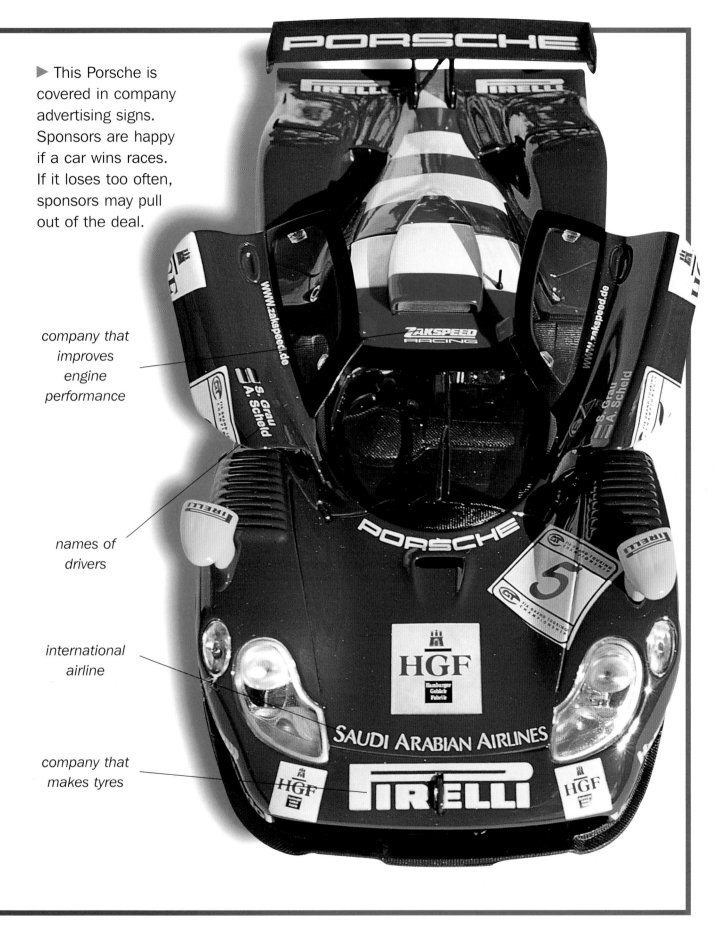

▶ This Porsche is covered in company advertising signs. Sponsors are happy if a car wins races. If it loses too often, sponsors may pull out of the deal.

company that improves engine performance

names of drivers

international airline

company that makes tyres

DRAGSTERS

A drag race takes place in a straight line. There is one quick blast down a 402-metre track, then the race is over.

▶ Rear-engined fuel dragsters have huge back tyres, and tiny ones in front.

Drag racing is a speed test between pairs of cars. They line up side-by-side in front of a traffic-light 'christmas tree'. Amber lights on the tree count down to green for 'go'.

With a mighty roar, the two dragsters hurtle down the drag strip. The fastest can do the run in under four seconds. By the end, they are moving at more than 500 km/h and have to use a parachute to slow down.

⚙ BURN-OUT BEFORE A RACE

For the best acceleration, a dragster's tyres need to grip the track well. Warm tyres grip better than cold, because warm rubber is softer and slightly sticky. Drivers usually do a burn-out before a race to heat the tyres. Water is poured under the tyres, then they are spun fast. The result is a massive cloud of smoke as the water boils and rubber burns! Then it is time to race.

▲ It's burn-out time before a race. As the tyres spin, they warm up, ready to give the best grip on the drag strip surface.

▼ A 'funny car' has a body based loosely on the style of an ordinary car. This one has its engine in front of the driver.

air intake to engine

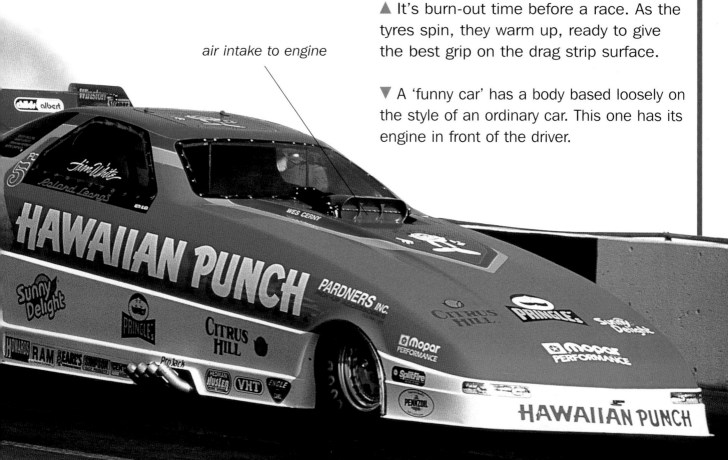

SOLAR CARS

▲ This solar car had a top speed of more than 140 km/h.

Since the 1980s races between strange-looking cars, powered by the Sun's rays, have become popular.

▲ The driver sits under a dark-tinted screen in the GM Sunraycer. The two 'ears' on top hold indicator lights and a system for seeing out of the back of the car.

Solar cars are almost pollution-free, because they do not burn fuel. Their power comes from solar cells, which change the energy in sunlight to electricity. This powers the electric motors.

Solar cells produce most electricity in bright sunshine, and then cars may speed smoothly along at 110 km/h or more. On a dull day, drivers have to rely on their batteries. When these go flat, few cars go faster than walking speed.

◀ Good weather for a solar race in Australia. Side-winds from passing trucks can be a problem for lightweight solar cars. All entries have to pass a test first, to make sure they won't be blown off the road.

The first big solar race was held over a 3000 km course across Australia, in 1987. Since then, the race has become a regular event, with teams from many countries taking part.

The cars come in many designs, but they all share a basic 'look' – a smooth shape to slip through the air easily, and lots of solar cells.

▲ This driver sits under a close-fitting plastic dome. The silver top reflects the sun's heat away from the driver's head.

▲ The 1999 Sunshark was built by students from an Australian university.

⚙ SUNLIGHT INTO ENERGY

Solar cells are usually made of a material called silicon. When light strikes silicon, an electric current is created. Wires from the solar cell can be connected to electric motors or batteries. Solar cells are used to power many machines, from calculators to satellites. Future cells may be strong enough to replace petrol engines in cars.

LAND SPEED RECORD

▲ Bluebird was a speed-record holder in the 1960s.

One of the biggest challenges in motor racing is the Land Speed Record, or LSR. Drivers are timed as they hurtle along on two runs.

Thrust SSC's driver sits in a small cockpit

Thrust SSC has two powerful engines, one either side

In 1997, a car called Thrust SSC went supersonic – it passed the speed of sound, at 1227.985 km/h. The driver was jet fighter pilot, Andy Greene.
To take the record, Andy had 1.6 km to get up to speed, then was timed whizzing along a further 1.6 km. Andy had to repeat the run going the other way within half an hour. Computer equipment confirmed that he was the fastest man on Earth.

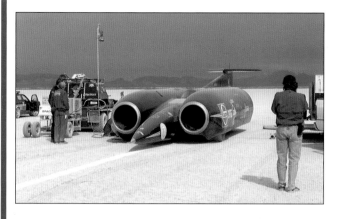

▲ Thrust SSC's engines are warmed up before the start of a test run.

▲ Thrust SSC's driver, Andy Greene, has a cramped cockpit, packed with controls.

▲ Thrust SSC has two jet engines. Before the car was built, they had been used in a jet fighter.

👁 BIG BANG IN THE DESERT

'We spent weeks in the US desert. Thrust SSC went a little faster with each test run. On record day, we saw the car hurtling along, then heard a double boom. We knew Thrust SSC was supersonic. The boom is made by an object going so fast it crushes the air in front into an air wave that we hear as a bang.' *Technician*

▲ Thrust SSC speeds across the desert, with the Black Rock mountains behind.

▲ Thrust SSC is towed back to the start line after each speed run.

FUTURE RACERS

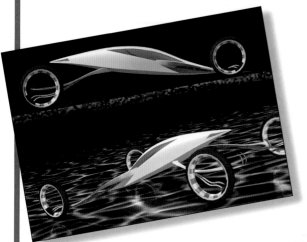

In future, racing cars may be built that are safer for drivers. Engines will make little pollution and will use less fuel than racers of today.

◀ In the future, designers may use new materials to build weird-looking machines.

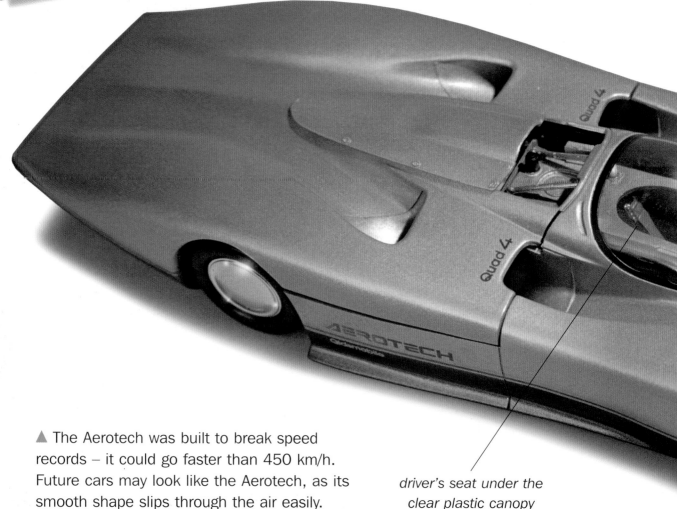

▲ The Aerotech was built to break speed records – it could go faster than 450 km/h. Future cars may look like the Aerotech, as its smooth shape slips through the air easily.

driver's seat under the clear plastic canopy

Today's racing cars use lots of fuel. A Formula 1 car covers only about one kilometre for every litre of fuel used. A small family car can go up to 20 times further on the same amount of fuel.

New rules could force racing car designers to develop engines that use less fuel, as well as power and speed. This should create cars that are better for the environment.

⚙ CLEAN METHANE

The petroleum liquid (petrol) we use as fuel comes from oil. When it is burnt, it creates pollution. In the future, scientists may work out a way to use methane gas. Methane is very clean-burning, with little pollution. Japanese researchers think they may be able to use huge amounts of methane that is trapped in rocks below the sea beds.

bodywork is built over a racing car monocoque

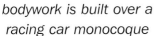

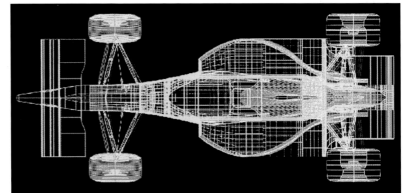

▲▼ Many racing car designers use computers to design cars. They can try out all sorts of ideas, before time and money is spent building the real thing.

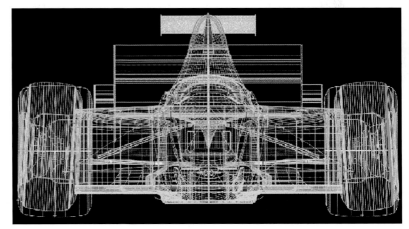

RACING CAR FACTS

Here are some facts and figures from the history of racing cars.

◀ Drivers in this 1937 race had little protection, apart from gloves and a lightweight helmet.

First race

The first known car race was held in the USA, from Green Bay to Madison, in Wisconsin. The route was 323 km long and was won by a steam-powered car.

Stopping to help

There were so many accidents in the 1903 Paris to Madrid race that it was stopped after the first day.

The only female in the race, Madame du Gast, became a heroine for stopping to give first-aid to injured drivers.

Deadly drive

In 1955 a car crashed at high speed during the Le Mans race. The driver was killed, and so were 82 spectators. It was the worst crash ever. Today, racing circuits have crash barriers. There is space between the cars and spectators. Ambulances and fire engines are always ready.

Grand Prix winner

The driver with the most Grand Prix Championships is Juan Fangio, from Argentina. In the 1950s he won 24 races, and was World Champion five times.

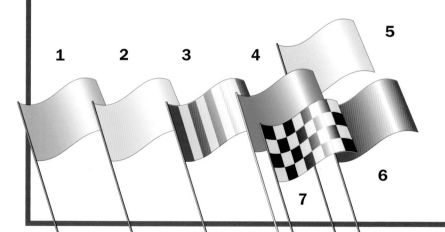

◀ Flags are used by officials to signal drivers during a race.
1 Car overtaking you, give way.
2 Danger on track, slow down.
3 Slippery track, probably oil.
4 Track now clear.
5 Slow service vehicle on track.
6 All cars stop at once.
7 Chequered flag, end of race.

A long way to go

Le Mans is a 24-hour race, so the faster your car, the further you go in that time. The greatest distance ever travelled was almost 5332 km, by a Jaguar in 1988. The car averaged more than 222 km/h.

Fastest dragster

The speed record for dragsters is held by US driver Gary Scelzi. In November 1998 he drove his car from a standing start to hit a top speed of 522.3 km/h, in just 402 metres along a drag strip.

Safety first

Safety equipment carried in a car includes seat belts, a fire extinguisher and a strong roll-over cage, made of thick steel. The roll cage takes the shock of landing, and stops anyone inside the car from being crushed.

Where's the steering wheel?

Grand Prix racing cars have such tight-fitting cockpits that the small steering wheel is removable. It has to be, otherwise there is not enough room for drivers to get in or out!

▲ Motor racing is an exciting sport, but crashes are common. Luckily, the driver of this car escaped with a few bruises.

A hot way to diet

Grand Prix driving is hot work, as the engine is just a short distance from the driver. On a warm day, the temperature in the cockpit can reach up to 50°C. During a race lasting perhaps 90 minutes, it's possible for a driver to lose more than 4 kg in weight, simply by sweating.

RACING CAR WORDS

Here are some technical terms used in this book.

front aerofoil

aerofoil
A wing-like part on a racing car that helps keep the car steady at speed. Unlike an aircraft wing, which lifts upwards, an aerofoil wing pushes down, forcing a car on to the track.

aluminium
A silvery-colour metal that is strong, yet light in weight.

banking
Angled trackside at corners, used on speedway circuits in the US. Like a cyclist leaning into a bend, banked tracks let cars go faster in corners.

burnout
A method of heating tyres for a drag race. Spinning the wheels heats up the tyres, which gives them more grip.

carbon fibre
The material used in bodywork and other parts of a car. Carbon fibre is usually a plastic with small hairs of carbon added. It is strong and light.

circuit
Any closed track used for racing.

cockpit
The area where a driver sits. Seat belts keep a driver in place.

◀ A racing car at speed, up on the banking of a US speedway circuit.

► A hoop (*arrowed*) protects the driver if the car rolls over.

crash barrier
Metal fencing that stops a car crashing into crowd areas.

ear defenders
Plastic cups like headphones, filled with material that absorbs sound.

formula
Rules that control how each type of racing car is made.

Grand Prix
French for 'big race'. The term usually refers to Formula 1.

monocoque
The centre body of a racing car.

petroleum
Fuel made from oil, a thick black liquid pumped from deep under the ground.

pit
The area where crews work on cars. Early ones were deep holes, dug to let mechanics work underneath cars.

pollution
Chemicals put into the air after fuel is burnt in an engine. An efficient engine makes much less pollution.

roll hoop
A metal hoop that sticks up behind a driver's head. If the car rolls in a crash, the hoop takes the shock of landing, so that the driver is protected.

scrutineer
An official who checks that a racing car passes formula rules, so that it can take part in a race.

solar cell
Silicon material that changes the energy in sunlight to electricity.

sponsor
A company that pays a racing team for advertising.

stock car
A powerful US car, based on a 'street' machine. In Europe stock cars are old cars that are raced on dirt tracks.

supersonic
Faster than the speed of sound. This is about 1220 km/h at ground level.

RACING PROJECTS

These mini-projects show you some of the science behind the world of racing cars and motor sport.

LOSING GRIP

Driving a racing car is a battle to keep the tyres gripping the track, especially in bends. Losing grip may mean a car skids off the track and crashes. In wet weather, water makes the problem even worse.

1 You need an eraser, a flat board and a jug of water. Flick the rubber across the board – it won't go very far before stopping.

rear aerofoil   *front aerofoil*

AEROFOIL ACTION

A racing car aerofoil works like an aircraft wing in reverse – it presses down, helping the car stick to the track. For this project you need a model car, thin card, sticky modelling clay and a bath of water.

1 Cut out a small card or plastic-sheet rectangle to make an aerofoil shape. Tape it carefully to the car's nose. Now fill the bath with 10 cm of cold water.

2 Angle the aerofoil upwards slightly. Release the car for a test run down the end of the bath.

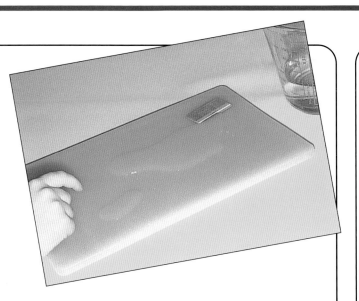

2 Now repeat, but wet the board first. You should see a big difference – the eraser loses its grip, and slides easily.

3 Water is thicker than air, so the test shows results at lower speeds than on a race track. At the aerofoil angle shown above the car lifts up. Try different angles to see which lift the car or press it down.

near the engine is the noisiest place to be!

SOUND LEVELS

Working in a race pit is noisy. Pit crews wear ear-defenders to protect their hearing. But how do noises compare? This list measures sound in EPNdB. Sound doubles every 10 EPNdB, so 50EPNdB is twice as loud as 40.

33	Rustling of leaves in a breeze
45	Whispering one metre away
72	Talking between adults
77	In a busy fast-food restaurant
100	Roar of traffic in a city street
105	Jetliner taking off overhead
120	Near a race car in a pit

INDEX